CAMEROON 2016 HUMAN RIGHTS REPORT

EXECUTIVE SUMMARY

Cameroon is a republic dominated by a strong presidency. The country has a multiparty system of government, but the Cameroon People's Democratic Movement (CPDM) has remained in power since it was created in 1985. In practice the president retains the power to control legislation. In April 2013 the country conducted the first Senate elections in its history, which were peaceful and considered generally free and fair. In September 2013 simultaneous legislative and municipal elections were held, and most observers considered them to be free and fair. In 2011 citizens re-elected CPDM leader Paul Biya president, a position he has held since 1982, in a flawed election marked by irregularities, but observers did not believe these had a significant impact on the outcome.

Civilian authorities maintained some control over security forces, including police and gendarmerie. President Biya is the commander in chief of security forces. Ministers-Delegate lead security and defense forces on a day-to-day basis but do not exercise total authority.

The most significant human rights violations continued to be killings and other abuses by Boko Haram in the Far North Region. These included child soldiering, abductions, beheadings, and burnings of persons and property. Other major concerns included involvement of security force members in torture and abuse; prolonged and sometimes incommunicado arbitrary detentions, often of suspected Boko Haram members; and denials of fair and speedy public trials.

Additional human rights abuses included disappearances, arbitrary arrests and detention, life-threatening prison conditions, use of unofficial detention facilities, restrictions on freedom of expression, including detention and harassment of and violence against journalists, and restrictions on movement. Corruption continued to be a severe challenge at all levels of government. Opposition and civil society activists were harassed, detained, and denied the right to assemble or operate by the government. Gender-based violence and discrimination, child abuse, and trafficking in persons remained problems, and harassment of and discrimination against members of the lesbian, gay, bisexual, transgender, and intersex (LGBTI) community, as well as the Baka and Mbororo minorities, continued. Violations of workers' rights were recurrent, and child labor remained a problem, especially in the informal sector.

Although the government took some steps to punish and prosecute officials who committed abuses in the security forces and in the public service, it did not often make public actual sanctions, and offenders often continued acting with impunity. The antiterrorism law was often used as justification by security forces to act with greater autonomy and less oversight by civilian authorities, at times leading to abuses with impunity.

Section 1. Respect for the Integrity of the Person, Including Freedom from:

a. Arbitrary Deprivation of Life and other Unlawful or Politically Motivated Killings

There were several reports security force members committed arbitrary and unlawful killings through excessive use of force in the execution of official duties, as a result of personal grievances, or through torture or other abuse of detainees. A June report by Amnesty International (AI) documented the deaths of six persons in custody following torture or mistreatment and the deaths of an additional four individuals in custody whose cause of death was unknown. Civil society organizations and newspapers generally blamed members of the three primary security forces--the Rapid Intervention Battalion (BIR), the Motorized Infantry Battalion, and the gendarmerie--as being responsible for the deaths.

On March 25, Moupen Moussa, a motorbike rider, allegedly died at a Secretary of State for Defense (SED) detention facility after gendarmes severely beat him for failing to produce his national identity card. According to reports, Moussa and another motorbike rider were returning from work late at night when a gendarme from the joint control unit stopped them and asked for identification. The officer physically abused Moupen and took the two to an SED facility, where gendarmes allegedly stripped them and beat them with a belt and baton. The gendarmes eventually released the second man after Moupen died. As of April 5, the responsible gendarmerie officer was allegedly in custody awaiting trial.

The terrorist network Boko Haram continued killing civilians, including members of vigilance committees and members of defense and security forces in the Far North Region. As of September 30, Boko Haram carried out at least 113 attacks in the Far North Region, which killed at least 262 civilians, 30 vigilance committee members, and at least six soldiers. There were numerous examples of abuses, such as the following: on January 13, a suicide bomber killed 13 during prayers at the Kouyape mosque, Kolofata subdivision, in the Far North Region.

Some abuses committed in 2014 and 2015 became public during the year. According to AI's June report, at least five of the 15 men arrested and brought to the Salak military base following a raid in Bornori in November 2014 died in custody, some as a result of torture inflicted by the BIR.

b. Disappearance

There were no reports of politically motivated disappearances. Nevertheless, there continued to be reports of arrests and disappearances of individuals by security forces in the Far North Region. In its June report, AI reconfirmed earlier reporting that since December 2014 at least 130 individuals arrested in Magdeme and Double remained unaccounted for. As of September 30, there was no news of the whereabouts of most of them. In its 2016 report, AI stated it had documented 17 additional cases of suspected enforced disappearances of persons accused of supporting Boko Haram committed by security forces in the Far North Region between April 2015 and February. As of June AI had not received a response to requests submitted to authorities about their whereabouts.

Boko Haram insurgents kidnapped civilians, including women and children, during numerous attacks in the Far North Region. Some of the victims remained unaccounted for.

c. Torture and Other Cruel, Inhuman, or Degrading Treatment or Punishment

Although the constitution and law prohibit such practices, there were reports that security force members tortured, beat, harassed, or otherwise abused citizens. According to credible nongovernmental organizations (NGOs), soldiers, police, and gendarmes tortured persons inside and outside detention facilities. Police, gendarmerie, and BIR officials reportedly detained and tortured persons in temporary holding cells in police, gendarmerie, and BIR facilities, and in cells located at the Directorate General for External Research (DGRE).

Police reportedly tortured detainees. For example, on February 4, Eyebe Levodo died while in detention at the legal department of the court of first instance in Yaounde. According to newspaper and NGO reporting, members of the regional delegation of judicial police arrested Eyebe on January 30 in the Yaounde neighborhood of Tongolo on suspicion of membership in a criminal gang. Police officers detained Eyebe on February 4 and referred him to the public prosecutor, a few hours prior to his death. At the mortuary of Yaounde central hospital, observers reported seeing bruises on his neck, wrists, shoulders, arms, ankles, and legs. In addition, they noticed Eyebe's mouth was swollen and there were other injuries to the head and other parts of the body, in addition to many other signs of trauma. The victim's sister allegedly told a journalist from *Kalara* weekly newspaper she received a telephone call from her brother who claimed that he had suffered horrific violence and that police used force to extort information from him. The public prosecutor opened an investigation shortly after the death. As of year's end, there was no publicly available update on the investigation.

On May 28, in Nom-Kandi, Ngan-Ha subdivision, Adamawa Region, four members of the fifth BIR tortured to death two young men named Abdou and Moussa. According to reports, villagers witnessed the torture but did not intervene because the soldiers were armed. The incident occurred after a woman accused Moussa of stealing 5,000 CFA francs ($9). Four BIR soldiers rushed to the suspect's residence, where they found him and Abdou. Moussa allegedly acknowledged the theft but pointed out that Abdou was not involved. The soldiers ordered both of them to get down on their knees and beat them. After Abdou and Moussa died, regional authorities, including the governor, confirmed the incident and claimed they had ordered an investigation. No information was released as of year's end.

AI's July report documented 29 cases of torture at the BIR military bases in Salak and Mora and at the headquarters of the DGRE in Yaounde. For example, Radio France International journalist Ahmed Abba was stripped and beaten while detained at the DGRE. Fifteen men arrested in Bornori were brought to Salak, where many of them were tortured and one died; four others later died in custody in Maroua prison. Other torture victims documented by AI described being beaten for long periods with sticks, whips, and machetes and stomped with boots, often with their hands tied behind their backs, as well as being slapped and kicked. AI documented the cases of six persons who died in custody following such torture.

Other government employees, including one teacher, abused children with disabilities placed under their custody (see section 6). During the year Mbuaye Manga Emmanuel, a staff member of the Bulu Rehabilitation Institute for the Blind in Buea, allegedly raped a dozen children with vision disabilities at the center. According to credible organizations, both public and nongovernmental, the victims were boys and girls ages seven to 17. They told police on May 28 Mbouehe had been sexually abusing them since 2014 and on several occasions he had forceful anal intercourse with them. Children said they had informed the director of the center, Jerome Nkwelle Ewang, but he did not act to help them. According to reports, barrister Mfontem Ozongashu eventually uncovered the abuses and filed a criminal complaint against the perpetrator with consent of the victims' parents. Preliminary investigations suggested the director helped the offender escape. The prosecutor remanded the director in custody for alleged complicity but granted him bail a few days later, and Ewang was able to resume work. As of September 10, the case was still open.

The United Nations announced in March that in 2015 there were 69 allegations of sexual abuse by peacekeepers in 10 peacekeeping missions around the world. At least one of these was committed by a Cameroonian peacekeeper in the Central African Republic (CAR). Reportedly new Cameroonian peacekeepers are required to sign individual commitment forms not to engage in sexual abuse as proof of the government's resolve in ensuring missions are carried out in good conditions, but their binding nature under the law remained unclear.

Prison and Detention Center Conditions

Prison conditions remained harsh and potentially life threatening due to gross overcrowding, inadequate food and medical care, and poor sanitary conditions.

<u>Physical Conditions</u>: Overcrowding was pervasive in most prisons, especially in major urban centers. Officials held prisoners in dilapidated, colonial-era prisons, where the number of inmates was as much as four to five times the intended capacity. Sanitation, food, and medical care were wholly inadequate. Authorities stated sick persons were detained separately from the general population; this was often not the case.

In January the country's prisons, which had an intended capacity of 17,000, held 27,997 inmates, according to the Ministry of Justice. Prisons in the Centre Region, with an intended capacity of 4,270, held 7,304 inmates. Those in the Littoral Region with a designed capacity for 1,550 held 4,250, while prisons in the North Region with a combined capacity of 1,300 held 2,776 inmates. At the individual prison level, for example, the Yaounde Kondengui Central Prison, with an intended capacity of 1,500, held 4,210 inmates; Maroua Central Prison, with an intended capacity of 400 inmates, held 1,486; and the Garoua Central Prison, with an intended capacity of 500, held 1,758 inmates.

Prisons generally had separate wards for men, women, and children. Unlike in previous years, there were no reported cases of officials routinely holding women in police and gendarmerie facilities with men.

As in 2015 physical abuse by prison guards and prisoner-on-prisoner violence were problems. In addition, "disciplinary cells" were often used to enforce discipline. Prison overcrowding led to a riot in one prison. According to media outlets and NGOs, on March 12-13, inmates of Garoua Central Prison launched a protest that developed into a mutiny. The prisoners were reportedly protesting life-threatening overcrowding, as there were nearly 2,000 inmates in the 500-capacity prison. Prisoners denounced lack of potable water and other inhuman conditions. Some detainees besieged the main prison courtyard and refused to return to their cells because of excessive heat and poor ventilation. The protest allegedly became violent when security force members attempted to return forcibly the prisoners to their cells. Three inmates died, according to official sources, and more than 40 wounded.

Overall, the quantity and quality of medical care, hygiene, and medicines was inadequate. Disease and illness were widespread, and sick inmates were not systematically and promptly separated from the general population due to lack of facilities. Malnutrition, tuberculosis, bronchitis, malaria, hepatitis, scabies, and numerous other untreated conditions, including infections, parasites, dehydration, and diarrhea, were rampant. In the Buea Central Prison, for instance, the infirmary contained four beds and a staff of four, including a doctor, a nurse, an assistant nurse, and a lab technician, some of whom were also expected to provide services to other prisons. Potable water and food were inadequate. Prisoners generally had one meal a day, and officials expected prisoners' families to provide additional food. There were reports of detainees using buckets as latrines in some temporary holding cells within police or gendarme facilities.

Corruption among prison personnel was reportedly widespread. Visitors were forced to bribe wardens to access inmates, and prisoners bribed wardens for special favors or treatment, including temporary freedom, beds, and transfers to less crowded areas of the prisons. Due to inability to pay fines, some prisoners remained imprisoned after completing their sentences or receiving court orders of release.

Many citizens in the North and Far North Regions turned to traditional chiefs for dispute resolution. In contrast with previous years, there were no reports of persons held in private detention facilities. There were, however, reports of the use of unofficial military detention facilities in the Far North Region, including on the BIR bases at Salak and Mora.

<u>Administration</u>: Recordkeeping on prisoners remained inadequate, especially in holding cells at police and gendarmerie premises where detainees often were not registered. Independent authorities often investigated credible allegations of inhuman conditions. Visitors needed formal authorization from the state counsel, failing which they had to bribe prison staff to communicate with inmates. In addition visits to Boko Haram suspects were highly restricted. Some detainees were held far from their families, reducing the possibility of visits.

<u>Independent Monitoring</u>: The government permitted international humanitarian organizations access to prisoners in official prisons; observers did not have access to prisoners held in unofficial military detention facilities. The National Commission on Human Rights and Freedoms and NGOs, including the Commission for Justice and Peace of the Catholic Archdiocese, made infrequent unannounced prison visits. The government continued to allow the International Committee of the Red Cross to make more regular prison visits. As in 2015 there were no reports human rights activists attempting to visit prisoners were required to pay bribes to prison officials.

<u>Improvements</u>: On July 12, the president enacted a law to amend the existing penal code, providing for alternatives to detention, including community service and reparative sentences to reduce prison overcrowding. Under the amended penal code, a person convicted of an offense punishable by a maximum of two years or a fine may be allowed to work for a public entity or compensate victims as alternatives to incarceration. Human IS Right, a Buea-based civil society organization, in partnership with Operation Total Impact, implemented a formal education and reformation education program in Buea and Kumba principal prisons.

d. Arbitrary Arrest or Detention

The constitution and law prohibit arbitrary arrest and detention. The law states that, except in the case of an individual discovered in the act of committing a felony or misdemeanor, the officials making the arrest shall disclose their identity and inform the person arrested of the reason. The law also provides that persons arrested on a warrant shall be brought immediately before the examining magistrate or the president of the trial court who issued the warrant, and that the accused persons shall be given reasonable access to contact their family, obtain legal advice, and arrange for their defense. The government occasionally did not respect these provisions.

There were several reports the government arbitrarily arrested and detained innocent citizens. In April, 63 individuals, including leading members of the opposition, were detained until late into the evening without charge, and at least one senior member of an opposition party sustained injuries from police handling. Government officials unofficially accused them of rebellion and inciting revolt, reportedly for organizing a campaign to wear black and distributing pamphlets. In October, 54 opposition members were again arrested at a political party meeting and detained for more than eight hours without being informed of the reason for their detention.

AI's July report indicated arbitrary arrests and detentions continued on a large scale in the Far North Region, and even the basic legal safeguards concerning arrest and detention were rarely respected.

Role of the Police and Security Apparatus

The national police, DGRE, Ministry of Defense, Ministry of Territorial Administration, and, to a lesser extent, Presidential Guard, are responsible for internal security. The Ministry of Defense--which includes the gendarmerie, army, and the army's military security unit--reports to an office of the Presidency, resulting in strong presidential control of security forces. The army is responsible for external security; the national police and gendarmerie have primary responsibility for law enforcement. The gendarmerie alone has responsibility in rural areas. The national police--which includes the public security force, judicial police, territorial security forces, and frontier police--report to the General Delegation of National Security (DGSN), which is under the direct authority of the presidency.

The government took some steps to hold police accountable for abuses of power. Police remained ineffective, poorly trained, and corrupt. Impunity continued to be a problem.

Civilian authorities maintained some control over the police and gendarmerie, and the government had somewhat effective mechanisms to investigate and punish abuse and corruption. The DGSN and gendarmerie investigate reports of abuse and forward cases to the courts. Lesser sanctions are handled internally. The DGSN, Ministry of Defense, and Ministry of Justice claimed members of security forces were sanctioned during the year for committing abuses, but the government provided few details.

On August 26, Captain Hamadjam Hamadjida Rene, commander of the Mokolo gendarmerie, Mayo-Tsanaga Division, Far North Region, was allegedly remanded in custody at the Kaele prison on a warrant issued by the government commissioner at the Maroua military tribunal. Captain Hamadjam allegedly played a role in a series of armed robberies targeting traders. He was relieved of his duties and immediately replaced.

The National Gendarmerie and the army have special offices to investigate abuse. The secretary of state for defense and the minister-delegate at the presidency are in charge of defense of sanctioned abusers. The minister-delegate of defense refers cases involving aggravated theft, criminal complicity, murder, and other major offenses to the military courts for trial.

Arrest Procedures and Treatment of Detainees

The law requires police obtain a warrant before making an arrest, except when a person is caught in the act of committing a crime, but police often did not respect this requirement. The law provides that detainees be brought promptly before a magistrate, although this often did not occur. Police may legally detain a person in connection with a common crime for up to 48 hours, renewable once. This period may, with the written approval of the state counsel, be exceptionally extended twice before charges are brought. Nevertheless, police and gendarmes reportedly often exceeded these detention periods. The law permits detention without charge for renewable periods of 15 days by administrative authorities such as governors and civilian government officials serving in territorial command. The law also provides for access to legal counsel and family members, although police frequently denied detainees access to both. The law prohibits incommunicado detention, but it occurred, especially in connection with the fight against Boko Haram. The law permits bail, allows citizens the right to appeal, and provides the right to sue for unlawful arrest, but these rights were seldom respected.

Arbitrary Arrest: Police, gendarmerie, and government authorities reportedly continued to arrest and detain persons arbitrarily, often holding them for prolonged periods without charge or trial and at times incommunicado. "Friday arrests," a practice whereby individuals arrested on a Friday typically remained in detention until at least Monday unless they paid a bribe to be released earlier, continued. There were several reports police or gendarmes arrested persons, without warrants, on circumstantial evidence alone, often following instructions from influential persons to settle personal scores. There were also reports police or gendarmes arbitrarily arrested persons during neighborhood sweeps for criminals and stolen goods or arrested persons lacking identification cards, especially in connection with the fight against growing insecurity, including the Boko Haram threat.

On April 22, in Esu, Mentchum Division, Northwest Region, at approximately 2 a.m., four gendarmes allegedly forced open the door to the home of Redemption Godlove, a high school teacher, seized him without warrant, and secretly detained him in Bamenda at the gendarmerie. On May 2, the gendarmerie referred Godlove to the state counsel of Mezam, who prepared a holding charge accusing him of "depredation by band" along with eight others and sent the accused to the examining magistrate of Mezam, who remanded Godlove in custody while conducting preliminary inquiries. The arrest was allegedly orchestrated by Baba Ahmadou Danpullo, owner of the Elba Ranch, who claimed the accused committed the alleged offenses. Godlove had served as spokesperson for Esu during a meeting with administrative authorities over a protracted land conflict with Danpullo. On May 31, the magistrate declined jurisdiction, claiming the state counsel of Mezam could not have jurisdiction since the alleged offense was committed in Mentchum Division, which has a high court, state counsel, and examining magistrate. The magistrate of Mezam canceled the remand warrant. The state counsel, however, kept Godlove in detention until July 14 when he complied, allegedly following the intervention of the attorney general of the Northwest Region.

Pretrial Detention: The law provides for a maximum of 18 months' detention before trial, but many detainees waited years for a date in court. In January the Ministry of Justice indicated that of a prison population of 27,977 inmates, 15,616 were in pretrial detention. Some pretrial detainees had been waiting for trial for more than two years. The increase in prison population was attributed to staff shortages, lengthy legal procedures, and administrative and judicial bottlenecks, including procedural trial delays and corruption.

For example, Oben Maxwell, an activist, remained in pretrial detention in Buea Central Prison, Southwest Region, as of August 31, where he had been detained since his arrest in 2014. The cited reason for his detention was holding an illegal meeting. The military tribunal initially handled the case; it was then assigned to the Buea court of first instance.

Detainee's Ability to Challenge Lawfulness of Detention before a Court: By law persons arrested or detained, whether on criminal or other grounds, are entitled to challenge in court the legal basis of their detention and obtain prompt release and compensation if found to have been unlawfully detained. There were no reported cases of challenges.

e. Denial of Fair Public Trial

The constitution and law provide for an independent judiciary. While the judiciary demonstrated impartiality and independence at times, it was often corrupt and subject to political influences. Individuals reportedly accused innocent persons of crimes or caused trial delays to solve personal disputes. As in 2015 there were no reliable reports that authorities disregarded court orders.

Over the past several years, Alhadji Baba Danpullo, a politically influential businessperson, used the judicial system to harass Musa Usman Ndamba, the senior vice president of the Mbororo Social and Development Association. The most recent episode of harassment was on April 27, when the examining magistrate at the Bamenda court of first instance committed Usman Ndamba and two others for trial over an issue that the court earlier dismissed in 2014. The magistrate charged them with propagation of false information and defamation of character, despite irrefutable evidence that he was not linked to the alleged offense.

The court system is subordinate to the Ministry of Justice. The constitution designates the president as "first magistrate," thus "chief" of the judiciary, making him the legal arbiter of any sanctions against the judiciary, although he has not played this role publicly. The constitution specifies the president is the guarantor of the legal system's independence. He appoints all judges, with the advice of the Higher Judicial Council. While judges hearing a case should be governed only by the law and their conscience as provided for by the constitution, in some matters they are subordinate to the minister of justice. For example, the Special Criminal Court must have approval from the minister of justice before it may drop charges against a defendant who offers to pay back the money he/she was accused of having embezzled. Despite the judiciary's partial independence vis-a-vis the executive and legislative powers, the president appoints all members of the bench and legal department of the judicial branch, including the president of the Supreme Court, and may dismiss them at will.

The legal system includes statutory and customary law, and many criminal and civil cases may be tried using either one. Criminal cases generally were tried in statutory courts.

Customary courts served as a primary means for settling domestic cases, including succession, inheritance, and child custody cases. Customary courts may exercise jurisdiction in a civil case only with the consent of both parties. Either party has the right to have a case heard by a statutory court and to appeal an adverse decision by a customary court to the statutory courts.

Customary court convictions involving alleged witchcraft are automatically transferred to the statutory courts, which act as the courts of first instance. The law provides for sentences of between two and 10 years' imprisonment and fines of between 5,000 and 100,000 CFA francs ($9-$170). There were no arrests or trials for alleged witchcraft reported during the year.

Customary law is deemed valid only when it is not "repugnant to natural justice, equity, and good conscience," but many citizens in rural areas remained unaware of their rights under civil law and were taught they must abide by customary law. Customary law partially provides for equal rights and status; men may limit women's rights regarding inheritance and employment. Customary law practiced in rural areas is based on the traditions of the predominant ethnic group and is adjudicated by traditional authorities of that group. Some traditional legal systems regard wives as the legal property of their husbands.

Military tribunals may exercise jurisdiction over civilians when the president declares martial law and in cases involving civil unrest or organized armed violence. Military tribunals also have jurisdiction over gang crimes, banditry, and highway robbery if such crimes are committed with firearms.

Trial Procedures

The constitution and law provide for the right to a fair public hearing, without undue delay, in which the defendant is presumed innocent, but authorities did not always respect the law. For instance, trials of Boko Haram suspects were sometimes not public. Defendants have the right to be informed promptly and in detail of the charges, with free interpretation as necessary from the moment they are charged through all appeals. They have the right to a presumption of innocence, but the government often did not respect that right, resulting in many pretrial suspects being treated as if they were convicted. Defendants have the right to be present and to consult with an attorney of their choice or have one provided at public expense, and the government generally respected this right, especially in criminal matters. Authorities generally allowed defendants to question witnesses and to present witnesses and evidence on their own behalf. Defendants have the right to adequate time and facilities to prepare a defense and not to be compelled to testify or confess guilt. Defendants have access to government-held evidence relevant to their cases, although in some cases the government did not make the evidence available in timely fashion. Defendants may appeal a conviction. The law extends these rights to all citizens, although they were not always extended in the cases of suspected Boko Haram affiliates.

On August 24, barrister Mohamad Al Amine of Maroua stated persons suspected of complicity with Boko Haram or being likely to compromise the security of the state were consistently tried by military court. He said the accused typically had no legal counsel and noted that, while the government commissioner assigned lawyers to defend them, the lawyers in turn assigned the cases to trainee lawyers, who received 5,000 CFA francs ($9) for legal fees. Often these designated lawyers were not allowed to access case files or visit their clients, which contributed to the poor quality of legal assistance. There were more than one hundred capital punishment sentences issued by the courts in the Far North Region between July 2015 and July 2016.

Political Prisoners and Detainees

No statistics were available on the precise number of political prisoners. Political prisoners were detained under heightened security, often in the SED. Some were allegedly held in the DGRE and at the Yaounde central and principal prisons, and the government did not permit access to such persons on a regular basis, or at all, depending on the case.

Former minister of state for territorial administration Marafa Hamidou Yaya, convicted in 2012 on corruption charges and sentenced to 25 years' imprisonment, remained in detention. On May 18, the Supreme Court reduced the sentence to 20 years. On June 2, the UN Working Group on Arbitrary Detention issued a decision qualifying Marafa's detention "a violation of international laws" and asked the government to immediately free and compensate him for damages suffered. The United Nations made it clear there were multiple irregularities in the judicial procedure.

Civil Judicial Procedures and Remedies

Citizens and organizations have the right to seek civil remedies for human rights violations through administrative procedures or the legal system; both options involved lengthy delays. There were a few reports the government failed to comply with a court decision on labor issues. For example, despite a court order, the government continued to work with the Cameroon Confederation of Trade Unions' former leader, who no longer represented the organization, to the detriment of newly elected officials.

Individuals and organizations may appeal adverse domestic decisions to regional human rights bodies. In 2012, for example, Jean-Marie Atangana Mebara, former secretary general at the presidency, filed a complaint against the government with the African Commission on Human and Peoples' Rights. Mebara complained the government was keeping him imprisoned on the basis of the Operation Sparrow Hawk Affair even though the Mfoundi High Court ordered his release. The commission delivered its verdict in April in Banjul, The Gambia. The commission directed the government of Cameroon to release Mebara immediately, compensate him 400 million CFA francs ($681,000) for damages, and punish all officials involved in the violations perpetrated on Mebara. The African Commission on Human and Peoples' Rights has no ability to compel a state to comply with its decisions.

Property Restitution

Over the past few years, to implement infrastructure projects, the government seized land occupied or used by civilians. The government failed to resettle or compensate those displaced in a prompt manner, leading them to protest in the streets on several occasions. In a few cases, corrupt officials misappropriated the money the government had earmarked for compensation. The government identified some offenders and opened cases against them. No particular group was reported to have been intentionally targeted for discriminatory treatment.

f. Arbitrary or Unlawful Interference with Privacy, Family, Home, or Correspondence

Although the constitution and law prohibit arbitrary interference with privacy, family, home, or correspondence, these rights were subject to restriction for the "higher interests of the state," and there were credible reports police and gendarmes harassed citizens and conducted searches without warrants.

The law permits a police officer to enter a private home during daylight hours without a warrant if he is pursuing a criminal suspect. Police and gendarmes often did not comply with this provision. A police officer may enter a private home at any time in pursuit of a person observed committing a crime.

An administrative authority, including a governor or senior divisional officer (SDO), may authorize police to conduct neighborhood sweeps without warrants, and this occurred.

Police and gendarmes sometimes sealed off a neighborhood, systematically searched homes, arrested persons, sometimes arbitrarily, and seized suspicious or illegal articles. In Wum, Northwest Region, on February 17, during an early morning raid following arson at the military barracks a few days earlier, police detained citizens without identification cards until identity could be established. There were several complaints police arbitrarily confiscated motorbikes and electronic devices.

Section 2. Respect for Civil Liberties, Including:

a. Freedom of Speech and Press

The law provides for freedom of speech and press but also criminalizes media offenses, and the government restricted speech and press.

Freedom of Speech and Expression: Government officials penalized individuals or organizations that criticized or expressed views at odds with government policy. Individuals who criticized the government publicly or privately sometimes faced reprisals. The government occasionally used the law requiring permits or government notification of public protests to stifle discourse, and many civil society and political organizations reported increased difficulty in obtaining approval to organize public gatherings. The government attempted to impede criticism by monitoring political meetings.

Antiterrorism legislation was also used to exercise government control over public and private expression. In November the military court of Yaounde sentenced three men to 10 years in prison for exchanging private text messages that joked about Boko Haram. The three individuals were not military personnel and were not accused of any terrorist involvement or support, but they were tried and convicted of "nondenunciation of terrorist acts."

Press and Media Freedoms: Independent media were active and expressed a wide variety of views, although there were restrictions, especially on editorial independence, in part due to terrorism concerns and the fight against Boko Haram.

Journalists reported practicing self-censorship to avoid repercussions for criticizing the government, especially on security matters.

<u>Violence and Harassment</u>: Police, gendarmes, and other government agents subjected journalists to arrest, detention, physical attack, and intimidation due to their reporting.

On May 17, a Voice of America (VOA) correspondent and state media Cameroon Radio and Television reporter, Moki Edwin Kindzeka, reported he was detained for four hours over a story he published on VOA speaking about crackdowns on corruption and some politicians' beliefs that President Biya was eliminating his political opponents. Unknown individuals forced Kindzeka into a car and interrogated, threatened, and offered him money for "favorable" reporting.

<u>Censorship or Content Restrictions</u>: The National Communication Council (NCC) is empowered to ensure all printed media comply with the legal requirement that editors in chief deposit two signed copies of each newspaper edition with the Prosecutor's Office for scrutiny within two hours after publication. Journalists and media outlets practiced self-censorship, especially if the NCC had suspended them. The NCC issued fewer warnings and suspensions than in 2015.

On July 14, the NCC issued sanctions ranging from warnings to temporary suspensions for up to six months. The weekly newspaper *L'Epervier* and its publisher received two suspensions of six and three months, respectively, for publishing unsubstantiated statements deemed likely to impair the reputation of persons, including Martin Belinga Eboutou, director of the civil cabinet of the presidency, and Eletana Ayinda Rene, another staff member of the presidency. Weekly newspapers *Ades-info* and *Le Regard* received three-month suspensions. Weekly newspaper *La Tornade* received a two-month suspension, while weekly newspaper *Canard Libre* received a one-month suspension. The daily newspaper The *Guardian Post*, weekly newspaper *Essingan,* and Roger Kiyek, Royal FM director each received a warning for unethical conduct, following complaints by some staff members of the presidency and the CPDM.

<u>Libel/Slander Laws</u>: Press freedom is constrained by strict libel laws. Any citizen may file a lawsuit against media organs for defamation of character. These laws authorize the government, at its discretion and the request of the plaintiff, to criminalize a civil libel suit or to initiate a criminal libel suit in cases of alleged libel against the president or other high government officials. Such crimes are punishable by prison terms and heavy fines. The libel law places the burden of

proof on the defendant. The government contended libel laws are aimed at safeguarding citizens whose reputations can be permanently damaged by defamation. The government and public figures reportedly used laws against libel or slander to restrict public discussion. While government officials and individuals filed libel complaints against media outlets with the NCC, none of the complaints was sanctioned with prison terms.

Internet Freedom

The government did not restrict or disrupt access to the internet or censor online content, and there were no credible reports the government monitored private online communications without appropriate legal authority. According to the International Telecommunication Union, approximately 11 percent of the population used the internet in 2014. Other studies stated the usage rate remained the same during the year.

Academic Freedom and Cultural Events

Although there were no legal restrictions on academic freedom or cultural events, state security informants reportedly continued to operate on university campuses. There were no reports the government censored curricula; sanctioned academic personnel for their teachings, writing, or research; restricted academic travel or contacts; intimidated academics into self-censoring; or attempted to influence academic appointments based on political affiliation. There were a few reports, however, of security personnel disrupting student activities. Further, the penal code adopted in July bans "political processions in any public establishment, school, or university"; it was criticized by some observers as isolating youth from the political process.

b. Freedom of Peaceful Assembly and Association

Freedom of Assembly

Although the law provides for freedom of assembly, the government restricted this right. The law requires organizers of public meetings, demonstrations, and processions to notify officials in advance but does not require prior government approval of public assemblies and does not authorize the government to suppress public assemblies that it has not approved in advance. Nevertheless, officials routinely asserted the law implicitly authorizes the government to grant or deny permission for public assembly. The government often refused to grant permits for assemblies and used force to suppress assemblies for which it had not issued permits. The government also prevented civil society organizations and political parties from holding press conferences. Police and gendarmes forcibly disrupted meetings and demonstrations of citizens, trade unions, and political activists throughout the year.

In the early hours of April 8 in Yaounde, the police Mobile Intervention Unit (GMI) detained 12 political activists at the judicial police headquarters for hours. GMI agents initially arrested the activists at the Biyem Assi neighborhood for wearing black, as they prepared for a distribution of pamphlets calling on Yaounde residents to observe a Black Friday, and took them to the GMI office in the Tsinga neighborhood. Edith Kah Walla of Cameroon People's Party (CPP) and Alain Fogue of Cameroon Renaissance Movement (MRC) went to the GMI to inquire about the others, and police detained them. Police subsequently transferred the detainees to the judicial police headquarters at Elig-Essono neighborhood and allegedly subjected them to humiliation for hours. Police took detainees' pictures, fingerprints, height, and shoe sizes before releasing them later in the day. Kah Walla and 53 CPP party members were again detained in October for more than eight hours, during which they were questioned without being informed of the reason for their detention. Speaking to media following their release, Kah Walla indicated the police arrested them with claims they were holding an illegal meeting.

Freedom of Association

The constitution and law provide for freedom of association, but the law also places limits on this right. The minister of territorial administration may, on the recommendation of the SDO, suspend the activities of an association for three months on grounds the association is disrupting public order. The minister may also dissolve an association if it is deemed a threat to state security.

National associations may acquire legal status by declaring themselves in writing to the Ministry of Territorial Administration, but the ministry must explicitly register foreign associations and religious groups; if they do not, the law imposes heavy fines for individuals who form and operate any such association. The law prohibits organizations that advocate a goal contrary to the constitution, laws, and morality, as well as those that aim to challenge the security, territorial integrity, national unity, national integration, or republican form of the state.

Conditions for government recognition of political parties, NGOs, or associations were complicated, involved long delays, and were unevenly enforced. This resulted in associations operating in legal uncertainty, their activities tolerated but not formally approved.

c. Freedom of Religion

See the Department of State's *International Religious Freedom Report* at www.state.gov/religiousfreedomreport/.

d. Freedom of Movement, Internally Displaced Persons, Protection of Refugees, and Stateless Persons

Although the constitution and law provide for freedom of internal movement, foreign travel, emigration, and repatriation, these rights sometimes were impeded. The government cooperated with the Office of the UN High Commissioner for Refugees (UNHCR) and other humanitarian organizations in providing protection and assistance to internally displaced persons (IDPs), refugees, asylum seekers, stateless persons, and other persons of concern.

In-country Movement: Police and gendarmes at roadblocks and checkpoints in cities and on most highways often extorted bribes and harassed travelers. Male refugees in Gado, for example, reported they were often required to pay between 2,000 and 4,000 CFA francs ($3.40-$6.80) when they traveled to Meiganga, even when they carried UNHCR-issued identification cards. Police frequently stopped travelers to check identification documents, vehicle registrations, and tax receipts as security and immigration control measures.

Exile: The law prohibits forced exile, and the government did not use it. Some citizens remained in self-imposed exile because they feared the government.

Internally Displaced Persons

Several thousand persons abandoned their homes in some villages on the border with Nigeria and fled to cities in the Far North Region because of frequent attacks by Boko Haram (83 percent of IDPs), while others left their homes as a result of natural disasters (13 percent of IDPs), mainly flooding. The July International Organization for Migration's (IOM) Displacement Tracking Matrix 4 for the Far North Region indicated the number of IDPs due to the conflict increased from 81,693 to 157,657 between April 2015 and July 2016. The total number of IDPs reported by UNHCR, including populations affected by natural disasters, was estimated at 192,912 as of September 30. Thirty percent of IDPs were children of school age, according to estimates by the UN Children's Fund (UNICEF). While IDPs were within communities spread across the entire Far North Region, Logone and Chari, with an estimated 91,131 IDPs (40 percent); Mayo Tsanaga with 24,258 (11 percent); and Mayo Sava with 45,386 (20 percent) were the three divisions that hosted most IDPs.

Protection of Refugees

Access to Asylum: The laws provide for the granting of asylum or refugee status, and the government has established a system of providing protection to refugees. UNHCR continued to play an important role in providing documentation and assistance to the refugee population. UNHCR and the government conducted biometric verification and registration of all refugees and asylum seekers in the Adamawa, East, and North Regions. As of September 30, 83,273 individuals, including 43,522 women and 39,751 men, had been registered. The country hosted at least 574,704 persons of concern to UNHCR as of September 30.

Refoulement: Following security measures taken by authorities in the Far North Region to counter Boko Haram, civil society organizations reported cases of forced returns, including individuals of Nigerian descent who spoke Kanuri. According to NGOs, persons speaking Kanuri were considered Boko Haram members or sympathizers and were systematically returned to Nigeria. UNHCR and government sources, however, did not confirm these allegations. Furthermore, 338 Nigerian asylum seekers arrived in early June in Kolofata, where UNHCR processed them for assistance. Cameroonian military authorities, however, unilaterally returned them to Nigeria.

Durable Solutions: The Cameroonian and Nigerian governments agreed in principle with UNHCR on the safe return of refugees who wish to be repatriated. Cameroon signed the agreement but awaited Nigeria's signature.

Temporary Protection: The government provided temporary protection to individuals who may not qualify as refugees, extending this protection to approximately 100,000 individuals during the year, including third-country nationals who had fled violence in the CAR.

Section 3. Freedom to Participate in the Political Process

The law provides citizens the ability to choose their government in free and fair periodic elections held by secret ballot and based on universal and equal suffrage. President Biya and CPDM members, however, controlled key elements of the political process, including the judiciary.

Elections and Political Participation

Recent Elections: In April 2013 the country held its first Senate elections. The ruling CPDM won 54 of the 70 elected seats; an additional 30 senators were appointed by the president, in accordance with the constitution. The elections were peaceful and generally free and fair.

In September 2013 the country held simultaneous legislative and municipal elections, with 29 parties participating in the legislative elections and 35 in the municipal elections. The CPDM won 148 of 180 parliamentary seats and 305 of 360 municipal council positions, representing slight gains for opposition parties, compared with the parliament elected in 2007. In preparation for the 2013 legislative and municipal polls, Elections Cameroon (ELECAM), whose members were appointed by the president, recompiled voter rolls using biometric technology and issued biometric voter identification cards that were required at polling booths. Despite irregularities, such as the inconsistent use of identification cards due to lack of expertise of local polling officials, opposition parties generally accepted the results. The high voter turnout (70 percent) and ELECAM's administration of the election were viewed as major improvements over previous elections.

In October 2011 President Biya was re-elected in a poll marked by irregularities, but one that most observers believed reflected popular sentiment.

Political Parties and Political Participation: The country had 300 registered political parties. Membership in the ruling political party conferred significant advantages, including in the allocation of key jobs in state-owned entities and the civil service. The president appoints all ministers, including the prime minister, and directly appoints the governors of each of the 10 regions, who generally represented CPDM interests. The president has the power to appoint important lower-level members of the 58 regional administrative structures. The government pays the salaries of (primarily nonelected) traditional leaders, which supports a system of patronage.

In the three elections held in 2013, the CPDM was the most popular party except in the Northwest, where it faced strong competition from the Social Democratic

Front. The CPDM remained dominant in state institutions, partially due to unfair drawing of voter districts, use of government resources for campaign purposes, interference with the right to organize and publicize views during electoral campaigns, and privileges associated with belonging to the ruling party.

Authorities sometimes refused to grant opposition parties permission to hold rallies and meetings.

<u>Participation of Women and Minorities</u>: There are no laws preventing women or members of minority groups from voting, running for office, and serving as electoral monitors, or otherwise participating in political life on the same basis as men or nonminority citizens. Cultural and traditional factors, however, reduced women's political participation compared to that of men. The law provides that lists of candidates for legislative and municipal elections should consider the sociological components of the constituency, including gender. Women remained underrepresented at all levels of government, but their political participation continued to improve. For the 2013-18 electoral period, women occupied 26 council mayor positions, in comparison with 23 in 2007-13, 10 in 2002-07, two in 1992-97, and one in 1987-92. Women occupied 10 cabinet positions, 76 of 280 parliamentary seats, and other senior level offices, including territorial command and security/defense positions. The Ministry of Women's Empowerment and the Family and civil society organizations such as More Women in Politics continued to promote women's political participation.

The minority Baka people took part as candidates in municipal and legislative elections but were not represented in the Senate, National Assembly, or higher offices of government.

Section 4. Corruption and Lack of Transparency in Government

The law provides criminal penalties for corruption by officials, although these were not always enforced in cases involving high-profile ruling party officials. The government increased anticorruption activities, including through integrating the UN Convention Against Corruption into the penal code enacted in July. Under the new code, different offenses are identified as corruption, including insider trading, involvement in a prohibited employment, and nondeclaration of conflict of interest. Reporting of corruption is encouraged through exempting those who report corruption to judicial authorities from criminal proceedings. Furthermore, corruption in official examinations is punished with imprisonment of up to five years, fines up to two million CFA francs ($3,390), or both. Nevertheless, corruption remained pervasive at all levels of government. The government did not always effectively address high-profile cases, and officials continued to engage in corrupt practices with impunity. The judiciary was not always free to independently investigate and prosecute corruption cases. In the context of the fight against Boko Haram, local sources indicated that corruption-related inefficiencies and diversion of resources from their intended purposes continued to represent a fundamental national security vulnerability.

Corruption: During the year the government sanctioned government employees for corruption, embezzlement, and mismanagement. Operation Sparrow Hawk, which was launched in previous years to fight corruption, including embezzlement of public funds, continued. The court opened new corruption cases and issued verdicts on some pending cases. Human rights activists and media reports, however, indicated many former officials ostensibly arrested for corruption had not been formally charged and that several had died in detention after not receiving proper medical attention. They claimed the government was using its crackdown on corruption as a pretext to target potential political rivals of the president.

In May authorities arrested a number of current and former government officials who allegedly played a role in diverting resources allocated for the compensation of Lolabe, Mboro, and Bongale populations in connection with the construction of the Kribi deep sea port. The officials included Jean Francois Vilon, former SDO for the Ocean division, now retired; Joseph Andre Edyebe, former assistant SDO for the Ocean division and currently divisional officer (DO) for Bagante; Hubert Bessala, former DO for Kribi I subdivision; and Ngoum, Ocean divisional delegate for agriculture, among others. As of September 30, the suspects remained in pretrial detention.

Although police were reportedly sanctioned for corruption, some officers convicted of corruption were relieved of their duties but retained their jobs due to weak oversight, accountability, and enforcement mechanisms for internal disciplining. Individuals reportedly paid bribes to police and the judiciary to secure their freedom. Police demanded bribes at checkpoints, and influential citizens reportedly paid police to make arrests or abuse individuals with whom they had personal disputes. There were reports some police associated with the issuance of emigration and identification documents collected additional fees from applicants. During the year the delegate general for national security, according to anecdotal reports, implemented measures to deter police officers from corrupt practices. Police officers found taking bribes were allegedly required to work without uniforms for a certain period, during which they had to serve as informants to denounce their colleagues as necessary.

Judicial corruption was a problem. According to press reports, judicial authorities accepted illegal payments from detainees' families in exchange for a reduced sentence or the outright release of their relatives. Judges were susceptible to executive influence and often delayed judicial proceedings in response to governmental pressure. In a few instances, the court avoided handling cases for politically motivated reasons. Many powerful political or business interests had virtual immunity from prosecution.

For example, after the DO for Bertoua I in East Region banned the meeting the MRC opposition party planned to hold on April 23, the party's lawyer, on April 20, filed a motion requesting the court cancel the DO's decision so that the MRC could meet on April 30. The law provides that in such circumstances, the court must issue a decision within eight days, but the court did not issue a decision until April 30. The court kept requiring additional paperwork until the MRC could no longer hold its meeting.

Overall, national anticorruption agencies helped recover an estimated 20 billion CFA francs ($34 million) of ill-gotten funds as of June 30.

Corruption in the education sector continued to be a major problem. Officials of major national training schools continued to be cited for corruption.

Financial Disclosure: The constitution and law require senior government officials, including members of the cabinet, to declare their assets, although the president had not issued the requisite decree to implement the law by year's end.

Public Access to Information: There are no laws providing citizens with access to government information, and such access was difficult to obtain. The National Institute of Statistics and other government agencies have websites that provide some level of information. Most government documents, however, remained unavailable to the public and media.

Section 5. Governmental Attitude Regarding International and Nongovernmental Investigation of Alleged Violations of Human Rights

A number of domestic and international human rights groups investigated and published findings on human rights cases. Government officials, however, impeded the effectiveness of many local human rights NGOs by harassing their members, limiting access to prisoners, refusing to share information, and threatening violence against NGO personnel. Human rights defenders and activists received anonymous threats by telephone, text message, and e-mail. The government took no action to investigate or prevent such occurrences. The government criticized reports from international human rights organizations such as Amnesty International, accusing the organizations of being biased and of intervening in security matters in a sovereign state without soliciting the government's point of view. Despite these restrictions, numerous independent domestic human rights NGOs continued operations.

There were several reports of intimidation of, threats against, and attacks on human rights activists, including members of the Network of Human Rights Defenders in Central Africa (REDHAC), OS-Civile Droits de l'Homme, and Front Line Fighters for Citizens' Interests (FFCI), amongst others.

For example, the intimidation of Maximilienne Ngo Mbe, executive director of REDHAC, continued. In February her landlord expelled her without notice from the house she had occupied for five years in Douala. The landlord claimed he was designated to become a traditional ruler and that authorities insisted his official coronation take place in Ngo Mbe's residence. As of August 31, however, the house remained unoccupied. In addition, on September 28 in Bafoussam, West Region, an unidentified person attacked FFCI member Nouayou Edy Michel and stabbed him in his left shoulder. The victim was returning to a hotel where he had an FFCI working session. The assailant did not take anything from Michel, who had two telephones and an important sum of money with him. Also, Mey Ali, president of OS-Civil Droits de l'Homme, continued to receive anonymous telephone and text-message threats, which compelled him to abandon his Kousseri residence and seek refuge elsewhere in the country.

Government Human Rights Bodies: The country has a national Commission on Human Rights and Freedoms (NCHRF), an independent institution for consultation, monitoring, evaluation, dialogue, concerted action, promotion, and protection of human rights. The NCHRF was established by a 1990 presidential decree and subsequently given more powers by a 2004 law. NCHRF powers are limited, however. It can only make recommendations to competent authorities. The commission publishes yearly reports on the human rights environment and may engage in research, provide education, coordinate actions with NGOs, and visit prisons and detention sites. As of September 30, the NCHRF had not released its 2015 human rights report. NGOs, civil society, and the general population considered the NCHRF to be a dedicated and effective organization, albeit inadequately resourced and with insufficient ability to effectively hold human rights violators to account. Its budget was far smaller than that of most other agencies with comparable status, such as the National Anti-Corruption Commission (CONAC) and ELECAM.

The National Assembly's Constitutional Laws, Human Rights and Freedoms, Justice, Legislation, Regulations, and Administration Committee was adequately resourced and effective in reviewing the constitutionality of proposed legislation. It approved most ruling party legislation, however, and was not an effective check on ruling party initiatives.

Section 6. Discrimination, Societal Abuses, and Trafficking in Persons

Women

Rape and Domestic Violence: The law criminalizes rape and provides penalties of between five and 10 years' imprisonment for convicted rapists. Police and courts, however, rarely investigated or prosecuted rape cases, especially since victims often did not report their cases. The law does not address spousal rape.

In the National Gender Policy Document for the period 2011-20 adopted in 2014 and released in 2015, the Ministry of Social Affairs and the Ministry of Women's Empowerment and the Family asserted 52 percent of women experienced domestic violence at least once and that 53 percent experienced violence by the age of 15. The ministries further indicated, based on a 2008 study on rape and incest, 5.2 percent of women were victims of sexual violence. Of those, 33 percent became pregnant and 16 percent contracted sexually transmitted infections. The report indicated more than one million girls and women were reported to have suffered an attempted rape and that rape was becoming widespread in all regions of the country. Included in this figure was incest, which applied to 18 percent of raped women.

The law does not specifically prohibit domestic violence, although assault is prohibited and punishable by imprisonment and fines.

The Ministry of Social Affairs and the Ministry of Women's Empowerment and the Family, in conjunction with local NGOs, continued their campaign to raise awareness of rape and educate citizens on penal provisions against rape, including through educative talks and sociolegal clinics. Activities were mostly centered on women commemorative days, such as the International Women's Day, African Women's Day, Rural Women's Day, and other fora involving mass mobilization of women. The Ministry of Women's Empowerment and the Family reportedly trained 150 police officers on how to address violence against women. During the year the Littoral branch of the NCHRF, in collaboration with Douala-based LFM Radio, implemented a program against gender-based violence. The interactive program broadcast every Saturday offered women the opportunity to share their concerns with, and seek advice from, a lawyer.

Female Genital Mutilation/Cutting (FGM/C): The law protects physical and bodily integrity of persons, and the penal code enacted on July 12 has specific provisions on genital mutilation/cutting. The law prohibits genital mutilation of all persons. Whoever mutilates the genitals of a person, by any means whatsoever, on conviction is subject to imprisonment from 10 to 20 years, and imprisonment for life if the offender habitually carries out this practice, does so for commercial purposes, or if the practice causes death. Children were reportedly subjected to FGM/C in isolated areas of the Far North, East, and Southwest Regions, in the Choa and Ejagham tribes, although the practice was reported to be decreasing. In 2015 The Ministry of Social Affairs and the Ministry of Women's Empowerment and the Family estimated the prevalence of FGM/C at 1.4 percent nationwide and 20 percent in the most affected communities. According to UNICEF's Global Databases 2016, FGM/C among girls and women ages 15 to 49 was 1 percent in urban centers and 2 percent in rural areas. In 2011 the government adopted a national action plan, and The Ministry of Social Affairs and the Ministry of Women's Empowerment and the Family established local FGM/C committees in areas where FGM/C was most prevalent, particularly in the Far North Region. The committees networked with former excision practitioners and traditional and religious leaders to reduce the practice. During the year the ministries and some civil society organizations conducted education programs against gender-based violence, including FGM/C.

Other Harmful Traditional Practices: The practice of widow rites remained a problem in some areas, especially in the south. The practices varied from area to area but generally entailed new widows having to remove all hair using a razor blade, spend the night sleeping on the floor, and forgo bathing and other hygiene practices for extended periods. Widows were sometimes forcibly married to one of the deceased husband's relatives as a condition for them to secure continued enjoyment of the property left by the deceased, including the marital home. In an attempt to better protect women, including widows, the government included in the new penal code provisions addressing the eviction of a spouse from the marital home by any person other than the spouse of the victim.

As in 2015, there were no credible reports of breast ironing, a procedure to flatten a girl's growing breasts with hot stones, cast-iron pans, or bricks. The procedure was considered a way to delay a girl's physical development, thus limiting the risk of sexual assault and teenage pregnancy. The procedure has harmful physical and psychological consequences, which include pain, cysts, abscesses, and physical and psychological scarring. During the year the government further discouraged the practice by including a relevant provision in the new penal code. Although the code does not specifically refer to breast ironing, it provides that whoever, in any manner whatsoever, interferes with an organ in order to inhibit its normal growth shall be punished with imprisonment from six months to five years, fines from 100,000 to one million CFA francs ($170-$1,700), or both. As formulated, the provision adequately covers breast ironing.

Sexual Harassment: The law prohibits sexual harassment. The new penal code provides punishment with imprisonment from six months to one year and with fines from 100,000 to one million CFA francs ($170-$1,700) for whoever takes advantage of the authority conferred on them by their position to harass another using orders, threats, constraints, or pressure in order to obtain sexual favors. The penalty is imprisonment for one to three years if the victim is a minor and from three to five years if the offender is in charge of the education of the victim. Despite these legal provisions, sexual harassment was widespread. Anecdotal reports suggest immigrant or refugee widows coming from the CAR were very susceptible to sexual harassment in the domestic work sector.

Reproductive Rights: Couples and individuals have the right to decide freely and responsibly the number, spacing, and timing of children; manage their reproductive health; and have access to the information and means to do so, free from discrimination, coercion, or violence. Many often lacked the information and means to do so, however, and societal pressures continued to reinforce taboos on discussing all sex-related issues, particularly in northern rural areas. Women's dependence on their husbands' consent was also a barrier to contraceptive decisions.

The UN 2014 Multiple Index Cluster Survey (MICS) indicated 82.8 percent of pregnant women had at least one antenatal care visit by a qualified health worker, 64.7 percent delivered with assistance from qualified birth attendants, and 61.3 percent of the deliveries occurred in a health facility. Prenatal care, skilled attendance during childbirth, emergency obstetric, neonatal, and postpartum care remained inadequate, particularly in rural areas.

Maternal mortality remained high. According to the World Health Organization's 2015 estimates, maternal mortality stood at 690 deaths per 100,000 live births. The high mortality rate was attributed to lack of access to medical care; lack of trained medical personnel; the high cost of prenatal care, hospital delivery, and postpartum care; and negligence by hospital staff.

For example, on March 12, the bloody and naked corpse of Monique Koumate and her twin babies were found on the ground at the Douala Laquintinie hospital yard; a relative had used a razor blade to open her womb in an attempt to rescue the unborn twins. Authorities claimed Koumate died hours before arrival at the hospital and blamed the sister who cut open her womb. The sister insisted she performed the surgery hoping to save the babies, who were still alive, because the nurses on duty refused to help.

The UN Population Division estimated only 20.2 percent of women and girls ages 15 to 49 used a modern method of contraception in 2015. The low rate of contraception use was largely due to the lack of skilled personnel and lack of adequate infrastructure and contraceptives. The Ministry of Public Health provided counseling services to women during prenatal visits, promoting the concept of responsible parenthood and encouraging couples to use contraception to space the timing of their children. The Ministry of Social Affairs also had an educational program on responsible parenthood, which was broadcast twice weekly. Couples were encouraged to get HIV/AIDS testing prior to conception, and efforts continued to increase HIV/AIDS testing for pregnant women at health clinics.

Discrimination: The law provides for the same legal status and rights for women as for men, including in terms of family, labor, property, nationality, and inheritance. Despite constitutional and legal provisions recognizing women's rights, women did not enjoy the same rights and privileges as men. For example, the law allows a husband to deny his wife the ability to work outside the home, and a husband may also forbid his wife to engage in commercial activity by notifying the clerk of the commerce tribunal. Also, while polygamy is authorized, polyandry is illegal. Customary law imposes further strictures on women, since in many regions a woman is regarded as the property of her husband. Because of custom and tradition, civil laws protecting women often were not respected. For example, in some ethnic groups women were precluded from inheriting from their husbands.

Although local government officials including mayors claimed women had access to land in their constituencies, the overall sociocultural practice of depriving women of land ownership, especially through inheritance, was prevalent in most regions.

The provision on adultery in the new penal code was revised to apply evenly to men and women. Under the previous law, a married man could be punished only if he had sexual intercourse in the marital home or habitually had sexual intercourse elsewhere with a woman other than his wife or wives. Under the new law, a husband who has sexual intercourse with a woman other than his wife or wives may be subject to punishment.

During the year the prime minister launched the UN Women initiative to involve men and boys in the advocacy against gender discrimination. The UN HeForShe campaign began on August 11 and aimed to engage men and boys as advocates and agents for change to achieve gender equality and women's rights.

Children

Birth Registration: Citizenship is derived from parents, and it is the parents' responsibility to register births. Parents must obtain a birth declaration from the hospital or health facility in which the child was born and complete the application. The mayor's office issues the birth certificate once the file is completed and approved. Because many children were not born in formal health facilities and many parents were unable to reach local government offices, many births were unregistered. According to the 2014 MICS, birth registration rate for children below the age of five was 66.1 percent. Social workers attributed the low level to negligence, poverty, and poor education. Parents often registered children only when the children were about to enroll for the first school leading to a certificate. A 2011 law brought innovations in the national civil status system, including creation in 2013 of a national civil status office that became operational with the appointment of its management staff in September 2015, but more especially the extension of deadlines for birth registration from 30 to 90 days, thus increasing the probability for parents to register new births.

Education: The law provides that primary education is compulsory but does not set an age limit. Children were generally expected to complete primary education at age 12, or at ages 13-14 if they had to repeat classes. In July the government criminalized interference with the right to education or training. Under the new penal code, any parent with sufficient means who refuses to send his child to school is subject to a fine of from 50,000 to 500,000 CFA francs ($85-$850), and imprisonment from one to two years if the offense is repeated. Public primary school was tuition-free, but children had to pay for uniforms, books, and sometimes extra fees. Secondary school students had to pay tuition and other fees in addition to buying uniforms and books. This rendered education unaffordable for many children. According to estimates from the 2014 MICS, the primary school attendance rate was 85.4 percent, with a primary school completion rate of 81 percent. According to a 2015 report from UNICEF, the Ministry of Health, and the National Institute of Statistics, 87 percent of boys attended primary school, compared with 84 percent of girls; and 55 percent of boys attended secondary school, compared with 50 percent of girls. According to the same report, 83 percent of boys completed primary school, compared with 78 percent of girls.

During the year Boko Haram destroyed hundreds of classrooms, and the government reportedly shut down entire schools due to security concerns. This aggravated lack of access to education in the Far North Region; the 2016-17 academic year was largely lost for many children.

Child Abuse: Child abuse remained a problem. Children continued to suffer corporal punishment, both within families and in the school environment. According to a 2011 survey, 76 percent of children reported being hit frequently at home, and 10 percent of those between the ages of six and 15 reported sexual abuse. Newspaper reports often cited cases of children abandoned, thrown in the trash, or being victims of kidnapping and mutilation. Also, Boko Haram abducted children and, in some instances, used them as suicide bombers.

For example, on February 16, in Buea, 14-year-old Nkeih Lizette reported her father Nkeih Ernest had been sexually abusing her since she was 10 years old. Nkeih claimed she had been pregnant four times and aborted three times using medications she bought on the streets. At the time she was suffering from severe hemorrhage, allegedly because of a failed abortion. The judicial police in Buea arrested the offender. There were no reported developments on the case as of September 30.

These allegations were consistent with findings of the International Center for the Promotion of Creation (CIPCRE), an international NGO. CIPCRE recorded 475 cases of sexual abuse of children from January 2015 to June 2016, including 36 children under age seven and 100 under 14. One hundred and nine children had contracted pregnancies, six died, 144 had severe injuries, and 49 were infected, all because of sexual abuse. In most cases CIPCRE stated the perpetrator was a relative.

On March 11, in Bamenda, Northwest Region, a four-year-old nursery pupil was discovered with serious scars on her face and body. NGO officials concluded the scars were a result of mistreatment the child received from her mother and a domestic helper.

Early and Forced Marriage: The minimum legal age for marriage is 15 for girls and 18 for men, although some families reportedly tried to marry their girls earlier. According to the 2014 MICS, 11.4 percent of women and girls ages 15 to 49 were married or in union by age 15, 36 percent of women and girls ages 20 to 49 were married or in union by age 18, and 22.3 percent of youths ages 15 to 19 were currently married or in union. Early marriage was prevalent in the Adamawa, North, and particularly Far North Regions. The government conducted education campaigns to combat early marriages and provided medical support and reintegration services to victims.

Female Genital Mutilation/Cutting: See information for girls under 18 in the Women's section above.

Sexual Exploitation of Children: The law prohibits the commercial sexual exploitation of children. A conviction, however, requires there to have been the use of threat, fraud, deception, force, or other forms of coercion. Penalties include imprisonment of 10 to 20 years and a fine of 100,000 to 10 million CFA francs ($170-$17,000). Penalties are increased to 15 to 20 years' imprisonment if the victim is 15 or younger, if a weapon is used, or if the victim sustains serious injuries as a result of trafficking. The law does not specifically provide a minimum age for consensual sex. The law prohibits the use of children for the production of pornography and provides for prison terms from five to 10 years and fines of five million to 10 million CFA francs ($8,500-$17,000) for perpetrators who use any electronic system to forward child pornography or any document that could harm the dignity of a child. Children under the age of 18 were exploited in prostitution, especially by promoters of restaurants and bars, although no statistics were available.

Child Soldiers: The government did not recruit or use child soldiers, but Boko Haram utilized child soldiers, including girls, in their attacks on civilian and military targets.

<u>Infanticide or Infanticide of Children with Disabilities</u>: Unlike in 2015, there were no credible reports of infanticide nor of mothers abandoning their newborns in streets, latrines, or garbage cans. The law criminalizes infanticide and provides penalties ranging from five years' imprisonment to capital punishment.

<u>Displaced Children</u>: The country hosted a large population of refugees and IDPs, most of whom were children. According to IOM's Displacement Tracking Matrix for August, there were 125,038 internally displaced children. This number excluded refugees. As in previous years, many children lived on the streets of major urban centers, although their number apparently declined as a result of stringent security measures against Boko Haram and the amended penal code that criminalizes vagrancy. The Project to Fight the Phenomenon of Street Children, a governmental project established in partnership with NGOs, continued to gather information on street children and offer health care, education, and psychological care but was hardly active.

<u>International Child Abductions</u>: The country is not a party to the 1980 Hague Convention on the Civil Aspects of International Child Abduction. See the Department of State's *Annual Report on International Parental Child Abduction* at travel.state.gov/content/childabduction/en/legal/compliance.html.

Anti-Semitism

The Jewish community was very small, and there were no known reports of anti-Semitic acts.

Trafficking in Persons

See the Department of State's *Trafficking in Persons Report* at www.state.gov/j/tip/rls/tiprpt/.

Persons with Disabilities

The law does not specifically address discrimination against persons with physical, sensory, intellectual, and mental disabilities in employment, education, air travel and other transportation, access to health care, the judicial system, or the provision of other state services. The constitution, however, explicitly forbids all forms of discrimination, providing that "everyone has equal rights and obligations." In 2010 the government enacted a law on the protection and promotion of the rights of persons with disabilities, but the president had not issued its instrument of implementation. In addition the country had not ratified international instruments such as the UN Convention on the Protection of Persons with Disabilities. The law requires new government and private buildings be designed to facilitate access by persons with disabilities and that existing buildings be modified to do so. Secondary public education is tuition free for persons with disabilities and children born of parents with disabilities, and initial vocational training, medical treatment, and employment must be provided "when possible," and public assistance "when needed."

The majority of children with disabilities attended schools. Some of these children attended mainstream schools, others attended specialized schools, including for children with vision, hearing, or physical disabilities. The Ministry of Basic Education started the 2016/17 school year by selecting 68 primary schools as pilot sites to implement inclusive education.

A private training institution, Shilo Special Education and Inclusive Bilingual Teacher Training Institute, which opened in 2014, continued training activities. As in 2015, the school accepted students with vision and other disabilities. In addition, the Ministry of Social Affairs has successfully partnered with NGOs, including Nicky's Foundation, a Baptist organization that works with persons with hearing disabilities and provides sign language training to teachers. The ministry also partnered with Sightsavers, an international organization, which worked in the Far North, South, and Southwest Regions.

National/Racial/Ethnic Minorities

The population consists of an estimated 286 ethnic groups, among which there were frequent and credible allegations of discrimination. Ethnic groups commonly gave preferential treatment to fellow ethnic group members in business and social practices. Members of the president's Beti/Bulu ethnic group from the south held key positions and were disproportionately represented in the government, state-owned businesses, security forces, and the CPDM.

Indigenous People

An estimated 50,000 to 100,000 Baka, including Bakola and Bagyeli, resided primarily in (and were the earliest known inhabitants of) the forested areas of the South and East. No legal discrimination existed, but other groups often treated the Baka as inferior and sometimes subjected them to unfair and exploitative labor practices. There were credible reports the Mbororos, itinerant pastoralists mostly present in the North, East, Adamawa, and Northwest Regions, were subject to harassment, sometimes with the complicity of administrative or judicial authorities, and were involved in conflicts over ownership of land and access to water.

The government did not effectively protect the civil or political rights of either group, but it implemented initiatives to promote the rights of the Baka, including the National Plan for the Empowerment of the Baka, and the Mbororo. Programs included training Baka and Mbororo in agricultural and animal husbandry techniques, including follow-on support for projects initiated after training, and recruiting Baka and Mbororo to attend teacher-training colleges. Baka and Mbororo communities complained about being marginalized, forcibly removed from their ancestral lands, and denied access to water.

The government continued efforts begun in 2005 to provide birth certificates and national identity cards to Baka. Most Baka did not have these documents, and efforts to reach them were impeded by the difficulty in accessing their homes deep in the forest.

To improve access for Baka children to education, UNICEF and the Ministry of Basic Education introduced an education model that takes into account the sociocultural specifics of minorities. They selected 12 schools to experiment with intercultural and multilingual education, in which the language of instruction is the mother tongue up to a certain level and then changes to the normal curriculum. The project was planned to run until 2017.

Acts of Violence, Discrimination, and Other Abuses Based on Sexual Orientation and Gender Identity

Homosexuality remained a crime. Consensual same-sex sexual activity is illegal and punishable by a prison sentence of six months to five years and a fine ranging from 20,000 to 200,000 CFA francs ($34-$340).

Although reports of arrests dropped dramatically, homophobia remained a major concern. Members of the LGBTI community continued to receive anonymous threats by telephone, text message, and e-mail, as well as social stigmatization, harassment, and discrimination, including threats of corrective rape, although they were increasingly reluctant to speak out. Both police and civilians reportedly continued to extort money from presumed LGBTI individuals by threatening to expose them.

For example, on June 1, human rights organizations reported management of the Real Estate Company of Cameroon ordered Franz Mananga, the executive director of Alternatives Cameroon, to vacate his apartment rented from the real estate company because his neighbors had brought a complaint against him for homosexuality.

Members of the LGBTI community allegedly suffered discriminatory treatment during a workshop held in Ambam, South Region, on September 1-4. The workshop was intended to train representatives of grassroots grantee organizations on the new funding model under the Global Fund to Fight AIDS, tuberculosis, and malaria. During the happy hour on the second day, hotel staff members discovered that gay men were involved. Thereafter, hotel staff members stopped replacing towels in all hotel rooms and reduced the quality of meals.

Despite the cultural environment, human rights and health organizations continued to advocate for the LGBTI community by defending LGBTI individuals being prosecuted, promoting HIV/AIDS initiatives, and working to change laws prohibiting consensual same-sex activity.

HIV and AIDS Social Stigma

Persons afflicted with HIV or AIDS often suffered social discrimination and were isolated from their families and society due to social stigma and lack of education about the disease. In the 2011 Demographic and Health Survey, 88 percent of women and 81.3 percent of men reported having discriminatory attitudes towards those with HIV. Between October 2010 and February 2011, Reseau Camerounais des Associations de Personnes Vivant avec le VIH (ReCAP+), a network of persons with HIV, conducted a survey of 1,284 persons with HIV. The survey indicated that in the 12 months preceding the study, 68.7 percent of respondents experienced at least one form of stigma and discrimination; 25.9 percent had been forced to change residence or were unable to secure rental accommodation; 22.6 percent of respondents who were employed lost their job or other income source; 6.7 percent were refused employment because of their HIV status; and 9.8 percent reported changes in their job responsibilities or being refused a career promotion due to their HIV-positive status. Two percent of respondents reported being denied health services, including dental care; 3.3 percent reported having been refused family planning services; and 5 percent reported being refused sexual and reproductive health services. During the preceding 12 months, 2.3 percent of respondents had been dismissed, suspended, or prevented from attending an educational institution because of their HIV status.

During the year there were a few reports of discrimination in employment. For instance, according to a credible NGO, the director of Societe de Production des Legumes (PROLEG), an agribusiness entity based in Bandjoun, West Region, terminated one of his employees because of his HIV status. Every year the director of PROLEG requires staff members to produce their HIV-status report. He allegedly terminated the worker after 27 years of service when the worker tested positive.

Other Societal Violence or Discrimination

There were a few reports of security forces failing to prevent or to respond immediately to societal violence. Several cases of vigilante action were recorded. For example, on May 4, according to newspaper reports, a bicycle rider and his colleagues entered Njo Njo cemetery in Bonapriso, Douala, where three suspects attempted to steal his bicycle. They caught one of the suspects and beat him to death. In another case, on May 7, in Bamenda, Northwest Region, residents discovered a burned body. Beside it they found a stone that was used to stun the victim and ash and debris from a tire the assailants used to burn him. According to reports, the incident occurred on the night of May 6-7, when the unidentified victim was caught attempting to steal a motorcycle.

On July 1, in Kumbo, Northwest Region, persons burned the feet of Ndzenyuy Ziawou and Nfor Arunna, two 13-year-old pupils of Islamic primary school Taakov, for allegedly stealing a woman's cell phone battery. Asana, the owner of the battery, allegedly called her husband and friends to discipline the children. They put the children on chairs with hands tied behind their backs and their feet tied to sticks fastened by the fireside. Using grass and firewood, they roasted the children's feet and abandoned them by a vacant building, where the children spent the night unattended. Hours after the severe abuse, Asana found the battery in her bedroom. The Justice and Peace Commission in Kumbo filed a complaint with the gendarmerie, which arrested five suspects and referred the matter to the Bui high court in Kumbo. The investigating magistrate opened preliminary proceedings on September 15, and the court delivered its verdict early December, sentencing two of the accused to one-year prison terms each. The other three suspects were expected in court on January 9, 2017.

Section 7. Worker Rights

a. Freedom of Association and the Right to Collective Bargaining

The law provides for the rights of workers to form and join independent unions, conduct legal strikes, and bargain collectively. The law also prohibits antiunion discrimination and requires reinstatement of workers fired for union activity. Statutory limitations and other practices substantially restricted these rights. The law does not permit the creation of a union that includes both public- and private-sector workers or the creation of a union that includes different or closely related sectors. The law requires that unions register with the government, permitting groups of no fewer than 20 workers to organize a union by submitting a constitution and bylaws, as well as nonconviction certifications for each founding member. The law provides for heavy fines for workers who form a union and carry out union activities without registration. Trade unions or associations of public servants may not join a foreign occupational or labor organization without prior authorization from the minister responsible for "supervising public freedoms."

The constitution and law provide for collective bargaining between workers and management as well as between labor federations and business associations in each sector of the economy. The law does not apply to the agricultural or other informal sectors, which included the majority of the workforce.

Legal strikes or lockouts may be called only after conciliation and arbitration procedures have been exhausted. Workers who ignore procedures to conduct a legal strike may be dismissed or fined. Before striking, workers must seek mediation from the Ministry of Labor and Social Security at the local, regional, and ministerial levels. Only if mediation fails at all three levels can workers formally issue a strike notice and subsequently strike. The provision of law allowing persons to strike does not apply to civil servants, employees of the penitentiary system, or workers responsible for national security, including police, gendarmerie, and army personnel. Instead of strikes, civil servants are required to negotiate grievances directly with the minister of the appropriate department in addition to the minister of labor and social security. Arbitration decisions are legally binding but were often unenforceable when parties refused to cooperate.

The constitution and law prohibit antiunion discrimination, and employers guilty of such discrimination are subject to fines of up to approximately one million CFA francs ($1,700). Nevertheless, employers found guilty are not required to compensate workers for discrimination or reinstate dismissed workers.

Industrial free zones are subject to labor law, except for the following provisions: the employers' right to determine salaries according to productivity, the free negotiation of work contracts, and the automatic issuance of work permits for foreign workers.

In practice the government and employers did not effectively enforce the applicable legislation on freedom of association and the right to collective bargaining. Although there were ministries tasked with upholding the labor laws, resources were inadequate to support their mission. For example, the city of Douala, which has six subdivisions, hundreds of companies, and thousands of employees, is part of the Wouri division with only one labor inspectorate, which was generally poorly staffed. Penalties for violations were rarely enforced and useless as a deterrent. Administrative judicial procedures were infrequent and subject to lengthy delays and appeals. The government and employers often interfered in the functioning of workers' organizations. The government occasionally worked with nonrepresentative union leaders to the detriment of elected leaders, while employers frequently used hiring practices such as subcontracting to avoid hiring workers with bargaining rights. Blacklisting of union members, unfair dismissal, promotion of employer-controlled unions, and threatening workers trying to unionize were common practices.

The Confederation of Workers' Syndicates of Cameroon (CSTC) held a congress in Douala on November 12-13, 2015, during which the organization elected new executive members, including Andre Moussi Nolla as president, to replace Zambo Amougou. CSTC officials immediately notified relevant authorities of the leadership change. In addition, a decision by the court of first instance in Yaounde suspended a parallel CSTC congress that Zambo Amougou convened on November 4-5, 2015. As of September 10, CSTC leaders claimed the government continued to consider Zambo as the official representative of the CSTC, inviting him to meetings and sending all CSTC correspondence to him, to the detriment of Andre Moussi Nolla and other new team members, despite multiple complaints by the CSTC.

There were reports of company officials prohibiting the establishment of trade unions in their businesses. For instance, officials of Union des Syndicats Libres du Cameroun (Free Syndicate Union of Cameroon or USLC), allegedly visited Dangote Cement Cameroon and Ciments d'Afrique, two companies established in Bonaberi-Douala, Littoral Region. USLC leadership claimed the managers were hostile to the idea of unionizing their employees and threatened retaliation against any employee who attempted to join the USLC. There were reports of other companies with no workers' representatives. FME-GAZ and COMETAL, for instance, reportedly sponsored only independent candidates during the March 30 social elections.

Some trade unions refused to acknowledge resignation of their members, in apparent collusion with their employers. For example, some employees of CRAFON, a Douala-based plastic manufacturing company, decided to leave the Confederation Syndicale Autonome du Cameroun (Autonomous Trade Union Confederation of Cameroon or CSA) to join the USLC. CRAFON management required them to have their letters of resignation endorsed by the president of the CSA, who refused to do so. CRAFON continued to pay the amount deducted from the salaries of these employees into the CSA accounts. In another case a trade union leader resigned from USLC and carried with him all of the USLC's documentation to join the Cameroon Confederation of Workers (CCT). The employer allegedly required all members of the USLC to follow their former president to the CCT. Despite their refusal, the employer reportedly transferred the amount deducted from their salaries to the CCT, thus forcibly transferring workers from one trade union to another.

Employers frequently used hiring practices such as subcontracting to avoid hiring workers with bargaining rights. Workers' representatives stated that most major companies engaged in the practice and cited the examples of ENEO, CDE, Cimencam, Guinness, Alucam, and many others. Subcontracting as a hiring practice was reported to involve all categories of personnel, from the lowest to the senior level. As a result workers with equal levels of expertise and experience did not always enjoy similar advantages when working for the same business, and the unprivileged typically lacked a legal basis to file complaints. More than 100 trade unions and 12 trade union confederations operated, including one public-sector confederation. On July 11, the Ministry of Labor and Social Security published the classification of trade union confederations by order of importance, following staff representatives' elections organized nationwide on March 1 and April 8.

A number of strikes were announced, some of which were called off after successful negotiation. Others, however, were carried out without problems, or with some degree of repression. Workers' grievances generally included poor working conditions, improper implementation of collective agreements, nonpayment of salary arrears or retirement benefits, illegal termination of contracts, lack of salary increases, and failure of employers to properly register employees and pay the employer's contribution to the National Social Insurance Fund, which provides health and social security benefits.

On May 17, management of urban transport company Transnational Industries Cameroon (TIC) Le Bus sealed off the company's offices, including its human resources, information, and finance departments, and attempted to forcibly expel employees from the company premises. Employees had been demanding payment of 14 months' salary arrears and several years of contributions to the National Social Insurance Fund (CNPS). Employees had sealed the door to the office of the company chief operating officer (CEO) in late April after he failed to comply with a previous agreement signed after a meeting with the regional labor delegate and the management of TIC Le Bus. Under the agreement the company management had to pay at least one or two months' salary by April 15. On April 19, the acting CEO offered only half of a month's salary, which the workers refused and demanded that he consult with the board chair. Meanwhile workers sealed the door leading to the CEO's office, seized the keys of his official car, and continued carrying out their duties.

Overall the social climate was tense, for diverse reasons. Retired workers were frustrated over perceived reluctance by the CNPS to comply with a February 15 presidential decree increasing pension ceilings. A briefing note from the CNPS stated the new rates would apply only to workers retiring in a year. Furthermore, the management of the CNPS in July 2015 allegedly issued a note indicating that occupational risk files being processed as of February 3, 2015, and that had not yet been approved by the authorizing officer may give rise to effective compensation only if the victim's employer had paid all social contributions to the CNPS. Trade unions also deplored the precariousness of jobs in subcontracting companies, especially on major infrastructure projects. They denounced the nonrespect of collective agreements in some sectors, including the media, private education, and security companies, among other sectors.

b. Prohibition of Forced or Compulsory Labor

The constitution and law prohibit all forms of forced and compulsory labor. The law prohibits slavery, exploitation, and debt bondage and voids any agreement in which violence was used to obtain consent. Violations of the law are punishable by prison terms of five to 20 years and fines ranging from 10,000 to 10 million francs ($17-$17,000). In cases of debt bondage, penalties are doubled if the offender is also the guardian or custodian of the victim. The law also extends culpability for all crimes to accomplices and corporate entities. Although the penalties were sufficient to deter violations, the government did not enforce the law effectively, due to lack of knowledge of trafficking and resources limiting labor inspection and remediation. In addition, due to the length and expense of criminal trials and the lack of protection available to victims participating in investigations against their offenders, many victims of forced or compulsory labor resorted to amicable settlement. The government, however, initiated a number of related criminal proceedings during the year and continued to place emphasis on street children considered most vulnerable to child labor, including forced labor.

There continued to be reports of hereditary servitude imposed on former slaves in some chiefdoms in the North Region. Many Kirdi, whose tribe had been enslaved by Fulani in the 1800s, continued to work for traditional Fulani rulers for compensation, while their children were free to pursue schooling and work of their choosing. Kirdi were also required to pay local chiefdom taxes to Fulani, as were all other subjects. The combination of low wages and high taxes, although legal, effectively constituted forced labor. While technically free to leave, many Kirdi remained in the hierarchical and authoritarian system because of a lack of viable options.

In the South and East Regions, some Baka, including children, continued to be subjected to unfair labor practices by Bantu farmers, who hired the Baka at exploitive wages to work on their farms during the harvest seasons.

Also see the Department of State's *Trafficking in Persons Report* at www.state.gov/j/tip/rls/tiprpt/.

c. Prohibition of Child Labor and Minimum Age for Employment

The law generally protects children from exploitation in the workplace and specifies penalties ranging from fines to imprisonment for infringement. The law sets a minimum age of 14 for child employment, prohibits children from working at night or longer than eight hours a day, and enumerates tasks children under 18 cannot legally perform, including moving heavy objects, undertaking dangerous and unhealthy tasks, working in confined areas, and prostitution. Employers were required to train children between ages 14 and 18, and work contracts must contain a training provision for minors. The Ministry of Social Affairs and the Ministry of Labor and Social Security were responsible for enforcing child labor laws through site inspections of registered businesses. The government employed fewer than one hundred general labor inspectors, whose responsibilities included investigating child labor. Although the government did not allocate sufficient resources to support an effective inspection program, workers organizations reported child labor was not a major problem in the formal sector.

The use of child labor, including forced child labor, particularly in informal sectors, remained rampant. According to the International Labor Organization's 2012 survey, 40 percent of children between the ages of six and 14 were engaged in economic activity; 89 percent of working children were employed in agricultural, 5 percent in commerce, and 6 percent in either industry or domestic work. Children working in agriculture frequently were involved in clearing and tilling the soil and harvesting crops, such as bananas and cocoa. In the service sector, children worked as domestic servants and street vendors. Children worked at artisanal mining sites under dangerous conditions. Children were also used as beggars. According to anecdotal reports, child labor was prevalent in the building construction sector, especially the use of refugee children. Chinese firms also reportedly resorted to child labor in the manufacture of children's shoes.

Parents viewed child labor as both a tradition and a rite of passage. Relatives often exploited rural youth, especially girls, as domestic helpers under the pretense of allowing them to attend school. In rural areas many children began work at an early age on family farms. The cocoa industry and cattle-rearing sector also employed child laborers. These children originated, for the most part, from the three northern and the Northwest regions.

Also see the Department of Labor's *Findings on the Worst Forms of Child Labor* at www.dol.gov/ilab/reports/child-labor/findings/.

d. Discrimination with Respect to Employment and Occupation

The law does not explicitly prohibit discrimination in employment or occupation based on race, color, sex, religion, political opinion, national origin or citizenship, disability, age, or language. The law does not specifically protect against discrimination based on sexual orientation, gender identity, HIV status, other communicable diseases, or social status. The constitution, however, states that all individuals have the right and the obligation to work.

The government generally attempted to enforce these legal requirements, but the large percentage of the population employed in the informal sector made effective enforcement difficult. Discrimination in employment and occupation occurred with respect to ethnicity, HIV status, disability, and sexual orientation, especially in the private sector. Ethnic groups commonly gave preferential treatment to fellow ethnic group members in business and social practices, and persons with disabilities reportedly found it difficult to secure employment. There were no reliable reports of discrimination against internal migrant or foreign migrant workers, although anecdotal reports suggested such workers were vulnerable to unfair working conditions. During the year, however, anecdotal reports highlighted only one case of discrimination with respect to employment, involving a West Region-based agribusiness entity. The government did not report publicly or privately on its efforts to prevent or eliminate employment discrimination during the year.

e. Acceptable Conditions of Work

The minimum wage in all sectors was raised to 36,270 CFA francs ($62) per month, up from 28,246 CFA francs ($48). The law establishes a standard workweek of 40 hours in public and private nonagricultural firms and a total of 2,400 hours per year, with the maximum limit of 48 hours per week in agricultural and related activities. There are exceptions for guards and firefighters (56 hours a week), service-sector staff (45 hours), and household and restaurant staff (54 hours). The law mandates at least 24 consecutive hours of weekly rest. Premium pay for overtime ranges from 120 to 150 percent of the hourly pay, depending on the amount of overtime and whether it is weekend or late-night overtime. There is a prohibition on excessive compulsory service.

The law mandates paid leave at the employer's expense at the rate of one and one-half working days for each month of actual service. A maximum of 10 days per year of paid special leave, not deductible from annual leave, is granted to workers on the occasion of family events directly concerning their own home. For persons under age 18, the leave accrues at the rate of two and one-half days per month of service. For mothers the leave is increased by either two working days for each child under six years of age on the date of departure on leave, where the child is officially registered and lives in the household, or one day only if the mother's accrued leave does not exceed six days. The leave is increased depending on the worker's length of service with the employer by two working days for each full period whether continuous or not of five years of service. For mothers, this increase is in addition to the one described above.

The government sets health and safety standards in the workplace. The minister in charge of labor establishes the list of occupational diseases in consultation with the National Commission on Industrial Hygiene and Safety. These laws were not enforced in the informal sector. The labor code also mandates that every enterprise and establishment of any kind, whether public or private, secular or religious, civilian or military, including those belonging to trade unions or professional associations, provide medical and health services for their employees. This stipulation was not enforced. The Ministry of Labor and Social Security is responsible for national enforcement of the minimum wage and work-hour standards. Ministry inspectors and occupational health physicians are responsible for monitoring health and safety standards, but the ministry lacked the resources for a comprehensive inspection program.

Despite the minimum wage law, employers often negotiated with workers for lower salaries, in part due to the high rate of unemployment in the country. Salaries lower than the minimum wage remained prevalent in the public works sector, where many positions required unskilled labor, as well as in the domestic work sector, where female refugees were allegedly vulnerable to unfair labor practices.

By law workers can remove themselves from situations that endangered health or safety without jeopardy to their employment, but authorities did not effectively protect employees in these situations.

www.ingramcontent.com/pod-product-compliance
Lightning Source LLC
Chambersburg PA
CBHW081252250726
48654CB00012B/1587